Put Beginning Readers on the Right Track with
ALL ABOARD READING™

The All Aboard Reading series is especially designed for beginning readers. Written by noted authors and illustrated in full color, these are books that children really want to read—books to excite their imagination, expand their interests, make them laugh, and support their feelings. With fiction and nonfiction stories that are high interest and curriculum-related, All Aboard Reading books offer something for every young reader. And with four different reading levels, the All Aboard Reading series lets you choose which books are most appropriate for your children and their growing abilities.

Picture Readers
Picture Readers have super-simple texts, with many nouns appearing as rebus pictures. At the end of each book are 24 flash cards—on one side is a rebus picture; on the other side is the written-out word.

Station Stop 1
Station Stop 1 books are best for children who have just begun to read. Simple words and big type make these early reading experiences more comfortable. Picture clues help children to figure out the words on the page. Lots of repetition throughout the text helps children to predict the next word or phrase—an essential step in developing word recognition.

Station Stop 2
Station Stop 2 books are written specifically for children who are reading with help. Short sentences make it easier for early readers to understand what they are reading. Simple plots and simple dialogue help children with reading comprehension.

Station Stop 3
Station Stop 3 books are perfect for children who are reading alone. With longer text and harder words, these books appeal to children who have mastered basic reading skills. More complex stories captivate children who are ready for more challenging books.

In addition to All Aboard Reading books, look for All Aboard Math Readers™ (fiction stories that teach math concepts children are learning in school) and All Aboard Science Readers™ (nonfiction books that explore the most fascinating science topics in age-appropriate language).

All Aboard for happy reading!

To Lori, Lisa, Kristin, and Anita for all
the fun years before the lightning struck.—J.D.

To my high voltage children,
Alex and Max—L.O.

Special thanks to Dr. Trace Jordan, Morse Academic Plan, New York
University.

Text copyright © 2002 by Jennifer Dussling. Illustrations copyright © 2002 by Lori Osiecki.
All rights reserved. Published by Grosset & Dunlap, a division of Penguin Putnam Books
for Young Readers, 345 Hudson Street, New York, NY 10014. ALL ABOARD SCIENCE
READER and GROSSET & DUNLAP are trademarks of Penguin Putnam Inc. Published
simultaneously in Canada. Printed in the U.S.A.

Library of Congress Cataloging-in-Publication Data

Dussling, Jennifer.
        Lightning : it's electrifying / by Jennifer Dussling ; illustrated by Lori Osiecki.
        p. cm.
        Summary: Introduces the wonders of electricity and lightning, including a look at what
    different cultures once believed lightning to be and how Benjamin Franklin proved what
    it really is.
        1. Lightning—Juvenile literature. 2. Electricity—Juvenile literature. [1. Lightning.
    2. Electricity.] I. Osiecki, Lori, ill. II. Title.
    QC966.5 .D87 2002
    551.56'32—dc21
                                                                        2002004739
ISBN 0-448-42860-1 (pbk)   A   B   C   D   E   F   G   H   I   J
ISBN 0-448-42877-6 (GB)   A   B   C   D   E   F   G   H   I   J

LIGHTNING

It's Electrifying

By Jennifer Dussling
Illustrated by Lori Osiecki

Grosset & Dunlap • New York

On November 9, 1965, a full moon rose into the dark sky over New York City. It was just after five o'clock. The city sparkled with lights in offices and apartments, restaurants and stores. Red and green streetlights blinked on and off as thousands of cars, buses, and taxis hurried through the city.

All of a sudden, everything changed.

Miles north of New York City, something went wrong in the giant conductor lines that brought power to the city. In minutes, New York City lost all its electricity. The lights went out. Elevators were stuck between floors. Subway trains stopped dead in their tracks.

There was a total blackout!

The entire city was shut down for over ten hours. Six hundred thousand people were trapped in the subway. In the Empire State Building alone, thirteen elevators remained jam-packed with people. The city's traffic lights weren't working. Cars didn't know when to stop or go.

And all because something went wrong with the electric power.

Until it is gone, most people don't realize how important electricity is. Think about your own house. How many things plug in? Lamps. TV. Microwave oven. Toaster. Stereos. VCR. Computer. Without electricity, none of them will work.

Electricity is the energy that runs many things in our everyday lives. It is hard to explain exactly what electricity is. And for something so important, electricity starts in a small way.

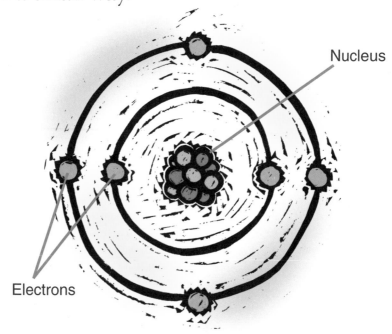

Nucleus

Electrons

Everything in the world is made of tiny bits called atoms. Houses. Trees. Food. Air. Water. Books. Animals. Even you! You are made of atoms. Electricity happens because of atoms.

Atoms are too tiny to be seen. Yet atoms are made up of even smaller particles. The particles have electrical charges. One kind of particle is called a nucleus. (You say it like this—NOO-klee-uss.) It is in the center of the atom. It has a positive charge. Other particles in the atom are called electrons. (You say it like this—ee-LECK-tronz.) Electrons have negative charges. The positive charge of the nucleus pulls at the negative charges in the electrons.

In some atoms, the pull is very strong. The electrons are held very tightly. Yet, in other atoms, the pull is weak. Sometimes the electrons can escape from the atom and travel to other atoms. This happens in certain metals like copper. A stream of electrons travelling through atoms of copper or other metals is what makes electricity.

Large power plants create electricity. Metal coils within giant magnets are turned by water or steam. This makes electrons run through wire and move from one atom to another.

The wires take this electricity from the power plant to towns and cities across the country. Some of these cables go right into your house. Just think—you are linked up to a huge power plant!

The wires that bring electricity to you are actually made of two smaller wires. One wire takes electricity into your house. The other takes it out of your house and back to the power plant. The cable is like a two-way loop between your house and the power plant.

If the loop is broken, electricity will not flow. That is what happened on a big, big scale in New York City during the 1965 blackout. This is also what happens every time you turn off a light switch in your house. That's because smaller loops connect the light switches in your house to the large loop. When you turn off a switch, it breaks the loop. Flip the switch on. The loop is complete again. The electricity can flow once more.

Most of the time, you do not see electricity. You only see what it can do. But there is one time when you can't miss it. That's because one type of electricity isn't made by power plants. It happens in nature. Can you guess what it is?

Lightning.

Lightning is a big, hot stream of electricity. One bolt of lightning is brighter than a billion light bulbs. It is white-hot. It travels at speeds of up to 60,000 miles per hour and one bolt can be from six to ten miles long. Yet it is only about as wide as your finger.

Lightning can start a fire on the ground. It can burn down a house. It can split a tree. If it hits a person, it may kill him. Each year, about 350 people get hit by lightning in the United States. That may seem like a lot. But there are about 287 million people in the country! It is very unlikely you will ever be struck by lightning.

Lightning can play some funny tricks. It can blow the clothes right off a person's back. Once it hit a man inside a sleeping bag and melted the zipper shut. Scientists don't know why lightning does such weird things. But they do know a little about what makes lightning happen.

Lightning begins in a big storm cloud. The cloud can be six miles high! Ice crystals and raindrops inside the cloud quickly move back and forth and up and down. All this movement makes an electrical charge in the cloud. The charge wants to escape from the cloud.

Meanwhile, in the ground under the cloud, another charge builds up. Scientists don't know quite why this happens. But they do know that the charge in the cloud and the charge in the ground want to meet. Sparks begin to shoot down from the cloud and up from the ground in streams. When the stream from the cloud meets the stream from the ground, it makes a lightning bolt.

This may be hard to understand. But did you ever rub a balloon against your hair? Do you remember what happens? When you take the balloon away, your hair stretches out toward the balloon. Both your hair and the balloon have an electrical charge. They want to meet up. The same thing happens between the cloud and the ground. And lightning bridges the gap.

The balloon and your hair have a kind of natural electricity. You have probably felt it another way, too. Sometimes if you walk across a carpet and touch a metal doorknob, you get a little shock. You may even see sparks. This kind of electricity is called static electricity.

Lightning is like static electricity. It jumps between a cloud and the ground like the sparks jump between your hand and the doorknob. But not all lightning jumps from a cloud to the ground.

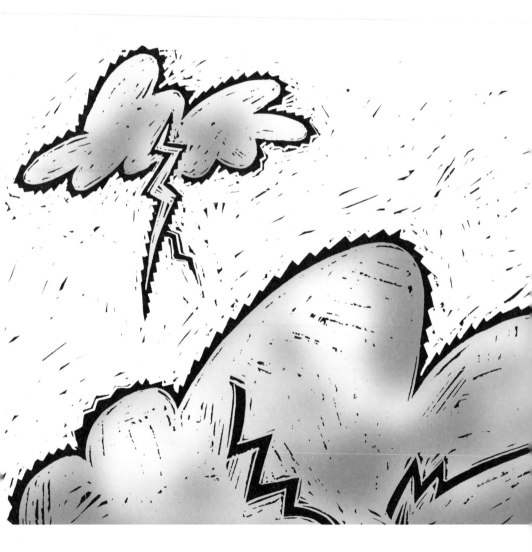

Lightning can hop between clouds.
Or lightning can happen within a cloud.
This is called in-cloud lightning. You may
have seen it before. The cloud flickers
with light and seems to glow from inside.

There is maybe one other kind of lightning. You will probably never see it. In fact, some scientists are not sure it even exists. No one knows what causes it. It is called ball lightning. Ball lightning is a bright spark that floats in the air. It is red or yellow and about the size of your head. Most lightning moves very quickly. Ball lightning moves much more slowly. It lasts a second or two and then explodes with a loud POP!

In the 1800s, a man told a story about ball lightning. A fiery ball floated into his house. It came toward him. It rose straight up, then it darted into a stovepipe and traveled through the chimney. At the top of the chimney, it exploded, knocking off chunks of stone and brick.

So how did anyone ever figure out that lightning is electricity? For a long time nobody made the connection. For thousands of years, people believed lightning came from angry gods.

The Viking people believed in Thor, the god of thunder. He had an angry temper. Lightning sparked when Thor struck his hammer against his anvil.

The Aztec people
of Mexico thought
that a god named
Tlaloc threw
lightning bolts.

In ancient Egypt,
Seth was the god
of storms and
lightning.

The ancient Chinese had a god named Lei Kung. He had wings, a bird head, and blue skin. He made thunder with his hammers.

In ancient Greece,
people believed that Zeus
was the king of all the gods.
He threw lightning bolts
at evil people from his
palace in the sky.

It took a long, long time for anyone to connect electricity with lightning. It was not until 1752 that someone proved that lightning was electricity. That someone was Ben Franklin.

Over hundreds of years, scientists had figured out some things about electricity. They knew electricity passed easily through metal. They also knew it didn't pass through things like silk and wax. Ben Franklin took this information and made up an experiment.

Ben was worried his experiment might not work. Ben was afraid other scientists might make fun of him. So he told his plan only to his 21-year-old son.

Ben found a large silk handkerchief and two sticks. He put them together to make a kite. Ben tied a pointed metal rod to the kite. He ran a long cord up to the kite. At the other end, Ben put a metal key. Then he tied a silk string to the end of the cord. Ben held on to the silk string. He knew the silk would keep the lightning from hurting him.

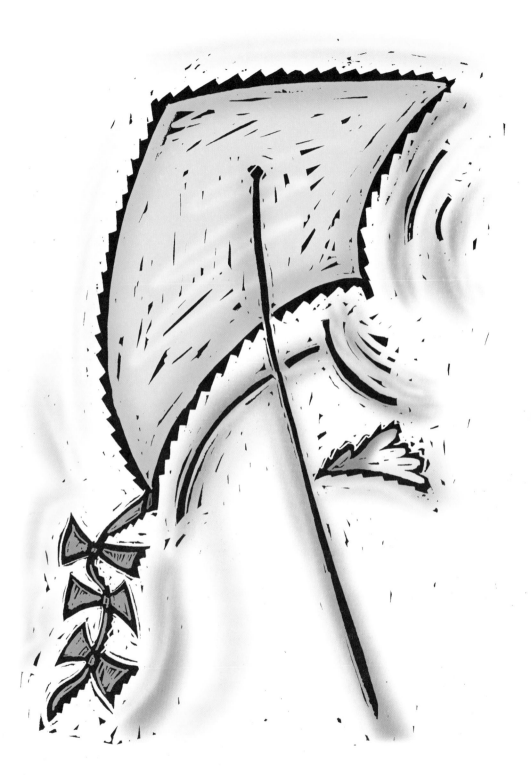

On a June day in 1752, Ben and his son saw a summer thunderstorm come up. They stood under a shed. The shed kept them—and the silk string—dry. From there Ben flew the kite. They waited for lightning to strike the kite.

When it did, it traveled down the cord. Just as electricity passes into

metal, the lightning passed into the
metal key. When Ben put his finger
near the key, a spark jumped to it.
(Don't try this!) Ben was a smart man,
but he did some very dangerous things!
However, with this experiment,
Ben Franklin proved that lightning
is electricity.

Because of his discovery, Ben was able
to make an invention that prevented many
fires. Most houses were made of wood. If
they got hit by lightning, the houses
caught on fire and burned down.

Ben knew lightning seeks a way to the
ground. It also usually strikes the highest
thing around. And he knew it passes easily
through metal. So in 1753, Ben Franklin
made the first lightning rod.

He attached a metal rod to a house.
Then he ran metal wires from the rod
down along the side of the house and
into the ground. The lightning rod
worked perfectly. When a thunderstorm
was overhead, lightning hit the rod, not
the house. The electricity then passed
down the wires and into the ground. No
one was hurt. The house didn't burn.

This idea explains why it's safe to be inside a metal car (with the windows rolled up) during a thunderstorm. The car is like a lightning rod. The electricity travels through the metal without hurting anyone inside.

But what do you do if you are not in a house or car during a storm?

Stay away from big trees and telephone poles and wire fences. Stay away from hills and open fields. Get out of any water. If you're stuck outside, crouch down. Don't lie down. Don't put your hands on the ground. If you put your hands on the ground, you would make a loop with the ground like the loop of wire that carries electricity to your house. Then the charge might pass through you to the ground and back up through you again!

One other place to avoid during a storm is a wet beach. But check out the beach after the storm is gone. You may find a fulgurite.

A what?

Fulgurites (FULL-geh-rites) are
sometimes called "fossil lightning."
They are twisted, crusty tubes of glass.
Lightning is so hot that when it strikes
a beach, it melts the sand into glass. The
biggest fulgurite ever found was in South
Amboy, New Jersey. It was nine feet long
and three inches wide.

Since lightning is very hot, it heats up the air around the bolt. The air expands quickly, then cools again quickly. This quick change makes a sharp crack. Can you guess what that is?

The sound is thunder. Sometimes you hear thunder the moment you see lightning. But sometimes you see a flash of lightning first and hear the thunder a couple of seconds later. That's because light travels faster than sound. So if the storm is near you, you will see the lightning and hear the thunder at the same time. But if the storm is farther away, you don't hear the thunder until a little later.

It takes the sound of thunder five seconds to travel one mile. You can tell how far away the storm is by counting the time between when you see the lightning and when you hear the thunder. Count "one Mississippi, two Mississippi, three Mississippi . . ." until you hear the thunder. (It takes about one second to say "one Mississippi.") So if you get to "five Mississippi," the storm is a mile away.

There are 44,000 thunderstorms every day on Earth. Every day lightning strikes millions of times. And lightning is not on Earth alone. Scientists think there is lightning on other planets, too, like Jupiter and Venus!

Electricity is all around us. Until a few hundred years ago, it was just a mystery. It was something people watched in the sky. It was something to be afraid of, something that could burn down a house. But today we know how amazing electricity is. It makes our lives easier. It makes our lives brighter.

At 4:44 in the morning on November 10, 1965, electricity returned to New York City. The subways started running. The elevators began to work. Street lights blinked red and green and yellow again. Most people were asleep when the power came on. But when they woke up, they were very happy to have it back.

So where would we be
without electricity?
In the dark!